Abstract

Equipment performance plays an important role in every industrial organization. Maintenance is concerned with the performance of a wide variety of activities needed for ensuring the smooth working of equipment and facilities. With increasing importance towards reducing wastes and maximizing productivity for manufacturing companies, optimizing the processes and machinery performance has become more critical than ever before. This needs a higher attention to be given to the reliability of the production facilities, to achieve good product quality at less cost. The maintenance and management of the company's production facilities is of increasing importance in modern factories. The measurement of their utilization will bring useful information about company performance. Total productive maintenance (TPM) is an equipment improvement effort, bringing maintenance and production departments together to prevent equipment downtime and failures. The fast rate of acceptance of TPM indicates that the practitioners always have the thirst for improvement in equipment performance.

The overall equipment effectiveness (OEE) measure is the basic requirement in a manufacturing industry improvement approach of TPM effort. Manufacturing organization can use the OEE calculations to know, how effectively the equipment is running. An accurate OEE percentage indicates whether the equipment is running at optimum capacity and producing quality output or experiencing unnecessary downtime. This study investigates and makes use of OEE performance measurement. The OEE measure basically consists of three factors namely availability, performance efficiency and quality The TPM activities will eliminate equipment losses related to availability, performance rate, and quality rate. Hence, the TPM implementation will increase the OEE value.

This project outlines the theories of TPM and OEE and implementation of the same in an automotive assembly plant. The automotive assembly plant entering in the mass production phase is struggling to achieve a decent OEE percentge. An attempt have been made to increase the OEE by using different lean tools and thus implementing TPM in an automotive assembly plant.

Key words:
TPM, OEE

List of Figures

List of Tables

Nomenclature

CMMS	Computerized Maintenance Management System
CMMS	Computerized Maintenance Management System
FDC	Fault Detection and Classification
MES	Manufacturing Execution System
SPC	Statistical Process Control
CPI	Continuous Performance Improvement
GIDC	Gujarat Industrial Development Corporation
JIT	Just In Time
JPH	Job Per Hour
OEE	Overall Equipment Effectiveness
OEM	Original Equipment Manufacturer
OPL	One Point Lesson
TEEP	Total effective equipment performance
TEI	Total Employee Involvement
TQM	Total Quality Management
TPM	Total Productive Maintenance

Chapter 1

Introduction

1.1 Introduction

The pressure on the markets is forcing companies to search for every possible competitive advantage over their competitors with target to find the potential in every process. A high performing production system is not only dependent on design but also on the processes of taking care of the system. This includes maintenance that aims to keep the system in an operational condition or bring it back to an operational condition after a breakdown and also ensures that the machine gives a good quality product. Thus giving the highest available time with zero quality defects and best performance of the machines. The above objectives can be fulfilled by a lean manufacturing tool called Total productive maintenance in a lean manufacturing plant. TPM stands for "Total Productive Maintenance" and builds a close relationship between Maintenance and Productivity, showing how good care and up-keep of equipment will result in higher productivity. It is a philosophy of continuous improvement that creates a sense of ownership in the operator(s) of each machine as well as in their supervisor. It is a process of maintenance management that empowers the organization with a progressive, continuous philosophy of enabling all manpower resources to work together to accomplish the mutual goal of manufacturing efficiency.

Modern manufacturing requires that the organizations that want to be successful and to achieve world-class manufacturing, must possess both effective and efficient maintenance. One approach to improve the performance of maintenance activities is to implement a Total Productive Maintenance (TPM) system (Hermann, 2000).Today, the competition has increased dramatically. Customers focus on product quality, delivery time and cost of product. Because of these, the company should introduce a quality system to improve and increase both quality and productivity continuously. Total productive maintenance (TPM) is a methodology that aims to increase the availability of existing equipment, hence reducing the need for further capital investment. Investment in human resources can further result in better hardware utilization, higher product quality and reduced labor costs (Chan, et al., 2003).

Now Overall Equipment Effectiveness is the key performance indicator in the Total productive maintenance which deals with availability of the machines, Quality defects and overall performance. Overall Equipment Effectiveness (OEE) and Total effective equipment performance (TEEP) are closely related measurements that report the overall utilization of facilities, time and material for manufacturing operations. OEE quantifies how well a manufacturing unit performs relative to its designed capacity, during the periods when it is scheduled to run. TEEP measures OEE against calendar hours, i.e. 24 hours per day. The main goal of the project is to obtain a best value to increase the production process in the company by using OEE.

Now in an ancillary industry to an automotive plant like Cosma International it is very important to carry out the current OEE and increase the OEE by deploying different TPM tools like preventive maintenance program, techniques, concepts and methods. The plant is located in Sanand GIDC. This facility builds body and chassis systems for multiple OEMs. Their main clients are Ford Motors and TATA Motors. This facility is spread across 356,000 square feet and employs more than 400 people. It began its volume production in July 2015. This plant specializes in Robotic MIG welding, Robotic Spot welding, projection welding and Bush Pressing. 61 BIW components and 3 Chassis components are manufactured. Maintenance is a very important area for providing production and the preventive maintenance is in fact, if used properly, a cost saver. This is of course also true for Cosma International where a stop in any machine is a large cost. When an event of this kind occurs, it is of great importance that the error is corrected as quickly as possible so that production can continue. Equally important is the quality of the product which should be considered as the company has the policy of zero defects and zero customer complaints. At Cosma International the corrective maintenance is called in when a machine is producing too low quality and has to be stopped or if the machine stopped on its own for some reason. And the machines and the processes should be calibrated in such a manner that the products manufactured does not have any defects and if any than it should be reduced to the extent that the same error does not happen again. Thus constant improvement in the process is required.

1.2 Problem Definition

Cosma International has a goal of meeting the cycle time dictated by the OEM, with minimum quality defects and maximum performance. There are a number of factors to improve productivity improvement in this auto ancillary industry and prime areas to be focused are number of products to be produced in stipulated time in order to meet the customer demand, identification of minor defects, process leaks and other parameters related to machine defects. Unplanned downtime plays a vital role. The causes for this include improper maintenance, lack of skilled workers and movement of semi-finished parts from one place to another. In the Ergonomic point of view the employee should be in a position to access all the parts as feasible as possible. More factory floor space is utilized. Material handling equipment find difficulty in movement of semi-finished parts from one layout to another owing to rough and uneven floor space existing in the factory floor. Moreover it has also been observed that the lack of co-ordination among the maintenance team increases response time. It is also required to ensure availability of the spares when it is required. Proper management system for spares availability is necessary.

1.3 Objectives

1. To study and understand the current maintenance techniques and strategies being followed at Cosma International and its contribution to the current OEE values.

2. To develop models, methods, concepts, strategies and practises for the implementation of TPM.

3. Implementation of the given TPM practises and calculation of OEE

Chapter 2

Literature Review

2.1 Literature review

The literature review has revealed that the manufacturing organizations worldwide are facing many challenges to achieve successful operation in today's competitive environment. Modem manufacturing requires that to be successful, organizations must be supported by both effective and efficient maintenance practices and procedures. Over the past two decades, manufacturing organizations have used different approaches to improve maintenance effectiveness. One approach to improving the performance of maintenance activities is to implement and develop a TPM strategy. The TPM implementation methodology provides organizations with a guide to fundamentally transform their shop floor by integrating culture, process, and technology[1]. TPM is considered to be Japan's answer to US style productive maintenance. TPM has been widely recognized as a strategic weapon for improving manufacturing performance by enhancing the effectiveness of production facilities[2]. TPM has been accepted as the most promising strategy for improving maintenance performance in order to succeed in a highly demanding market arena[1]. TPM is the proven manufacturing strategy that has been successfully employed globally for the last three decades, for achieving the organizational objectives of achieving core competence in the competitive environment (Ahuja et al., 2004)[3]. TPM is a highly influential technique that is in the core of "operations management" and deserves immediate attention by organizations across the globe[4].TPM is a methodology originating from Japan to support its lean manufacturing system, since dependable and effective equipment are essential pre-requisite for implementing Lean manufacturing initiatives in the organizations[5]. While Just-In-Time (JIT) and (TQM) programs have been around for a while, the manufacturing organizations off late, have been putting in enough confidence upon the latest strategic quality maintenance tool as TPM. Figure 1shows the relationships between TPM and Lean Manufacturing building blocks. It is clearly revealed, that TPM is the corner stone activity for most of the lean manufacturing philosophies and can effectively contribute towards success of lean manufacturing.

TPM is a production-driven improvement methodology that is designed to optimize equipment reliability and ensure efficient management of plant assets[6]. TPM is a change philosophy, which has contributed significantly towards realization of significant improvements in the manufacturing organizations in the West and Japan (Maggard and Rhyne, 1992). TPM has been depicted as a manufacturing strategy comprising of following steps (Nakajima, 1989; Bamber et al.,1999; Suzuki, 1992)[7]:maximizing equipment effectiveness through optimization of equipment availability, performance, efficiency and product quality; establishing a preventive maintenance strategy for the entire life cycle of equipment; covering all departments such as planning, user and maintenance departments.

Figure 2.1: TPM Big losses

As shown in figure 2.1 here six big losses of TPM is shown which reduces the overall OEE percentage. Nakajima (1989), a major contributor of TPM, has defined TPM as an innovative approach to maintenance that optimizes equipment effectiveness, eliminates breakdowns, and promotes autonomous maintenance by operators through day-to-day activities involving the total workforce[7]. The emergence of TPM is intended to bring both production and maintenance functions together by a combination of good working practices, team-working and continuous improvement[7]. Willmott (1994) portrays TPM as a relatively new and practical application of TQM and suggests that TPM aims to promote a culture in which operators develop "ownership" of their machines, learn much more about them, and in the process realize skilled trades to concentrate on problem diagnostic and equipment improvement projects. TPM is not a maintenance specific policy, it is a culture, a philosophy and a new attitude towards maintenance[8]. TPM is a system (culture) that takes advantage of the abilities and skills of all individuals in an organization[9]. An effective TPM implementation program provides for a philosophy based upon the empowerment and encouragement of personnel from all areas in the organization[1].TPM is about communication. It mandates that operators, maintenance people and engineers collectively collaborate and understand each other's language (Witt, 2006)[8].

TPM describes a synergistic relationship among all organizational functions, but particularly between production and maintenance, for the continuous improvement of product quality, operational efficiency, productivity and safety[10]. According to Chaneski (2002), TPM is a maintenance management programme with the objective of eliminating equipment downtime. TPM is an innovative approach to plant maintenance that is complementary to Total Quality Management (TQM), Just-in-Time Manufacturing (JIT), (TEI), (CPI), and other world-class manufacturing strategies[11]. Lawrence (1999) describes TPM as the general movement on the part of businesses to try to do more with fewer resources. According to Besterfieldet al.(1999)[9], TPM helps to maintain the current plant and equipment at its highest productive level through the cooperation of all functional areas of an organization. TPM is designed to maximize the overall equipment effectiveness. It involves all departments that plan, use and maintain equipment, involves all employees from top management to front line workers. The concept of TPM was developed in Denso, A tier one automotive supplier in the Toyota group of suppliers, during 1960s and 70s in Japan. The central thrust of the programme was the complete elimination of the "six major equipment losses". The key concept behind effective improvements was autonomous maintenance. The concept of overall equipment effectiveness (OEE) and focused improvement were found to be quite encouraging for success of TPM. The aim of the TPM is to improve the labor productivity and to reduce the maintenance cost. The work of the Japanese consultant Koichi in Nissan Motors were acknowledged as 10% reduction in maintenance cost, 30% reduction in manpower and 140% increase in labor productivity were reported. Author reported that labor productivity increases by 140%-150% and maintenance cost decreases by 15%. Customers claim that poor quality reduces

2.2 TPM as a Performance Measurement System

The maintenance strategy involving all those activities to improve equipment productivity by performing Preventive Maintenance, Corrective Maintenance, and Maintenance Prevention throughout the life cycle of equipment is called 'Productive Maintenance'.[1]. Total Productive Maintenance (TPM) is an innovative approach to maintenance that optimizes equipment effectiveness, eliminates breakdowns and promotes autonomous maintenance by operators through day-to-day activities involving total workforce. TPM is based on three interrelated concepts: (i) maximizing equipment effectiveness; (ii) autonomous maintenance by operators; and (iii) small group activities[12]. TPM is designed to maximize equipment effectiveness (improving overall efficiency) by establishing a comprehensive productive maintenance system covering the entire life of the equipment, spanning all equipment-related fields (planning, use, maintenance, etc.) and, with the participation of all employees from top management down to shop-floor workers, to promote productive maintenance through motivation management or voluntary small-group activities[13]. TPM describes a synergistic relationship among all organizational functions, but particularly between production and maintenance, for the continuous improvement of product quality, operational efficiency, productivity and safety[14]. TPM has been accepted as the most promising strategy for improving maintenance performance in order to succeed in a highly demanding market arena. Total Productive Maintenance is a proven17 manufacturing strategy that has been successfully employed globally for the past three decades, for achieving the organizational objectives of achieving core competence in the competitive environment[10]. TPM has been widely recognized as a strategic weapon for improving manufacturing performance by enhancing the effectiveness of production facilities[11].

2.3   Need for TPM in Manufacturing Scenario

According to Nakajima (1988), Total Productive Maintenance when implemented fully, dramatically improves productivity and quality, and reduces costs. TPM is not a maintenance specific policy; it is a culture, a philosophy and a new attitude towards maintenance[12]. It is a system that takes advantage of the abilities and skills of all individuals in an organization. TPM is an innovative approach to plant maintenance that is complementary to Total Quality Management, Just-in-Time Manufacturing, Total Employee Involvement, Continuous Performance Improvement, and other world-class manufacturing strategies[13]. TPM also succeeded well in making maintenance into an overall companywide issue, by focusing on continuous improvements, autonomous small group activities, training, education, communication and the flow of information[14].

One of the main aims of TPM is to increase the productivity of plant with only a modest investment in maintenance[15]. The emergence of TPM is intended to bring both production and maintenance functions together by a combination of good working practices, team-working and continuous improvement[15]. The study conducted by Brah and Chong (2004) focused on gaining insights into the impact of TPM on the performance of the organization. There is a support for a positive correlation between TPM and business performance[16].

Total productive maintenance is a methodology that aims to increase the availability of existing equipment hence reducing the need for further capital investment. Investment in human resources can further result in better hardware utilization, higher product quality and reduced labour costs[17]. Ahmed (2005) stated that a well-drawn TPM implementation plan not only improves equipment efficiency and effectiveness but also brings appreciable improvements in other areas such as reduction of manufacturing cycle time, size of inventory, customer complaints, and creates cohesive small group autonomous teams and increases the skill and confidence of individuals. TPM not only leads to increase in efficiency and effectiveness of manufacturing systems, measured in terms of OEE index, by reducing the wastages but also prepares the plant to meet the challenges put forward by globally competing economies to achieve world class manufacturing status[18]. With the achievements of zero breakdowns, zero accidents and zero defects, operators get new confidence in their own abilities and the organizations also realize the importance of employee contributions towards the realization of manufacturing performance[19].

2.4 OEE as a Maintenance Performance Measure

Due to intense global competition, companies are striving to improve and optimize their productivity in order to stay competitive. This situation has led to the need for more rigorously defined productivity metrics that are able to take into account several important factors, such as equipment availability (breakdowns, set-ups and adjustments), performance (reduced speed, idling and minor stoppages), and quality (defects, rework and yield)[20]. Campbell (1995) has classified the commonly used measure of maintenance performance into three categories on the basis of their focus; viz. measures of equipment performance – e.g. availability, reliability, overall equipment effectiveness; measures of cost performance – e.g. operation & maintenance labour and material costs; measures of process performance – e.g. ratio of planned and unplanned work, schedule compliance.

The total productive maintenance concept has provided a quantitative metric, Overall Equipment Effectiveness for measuring the productivity of individual production equipment in a factory. According to[18] one of the important contributions of OEE is to consider equipment's hidden losses in computing equipment utilization. Before the advent of OEE, only availability was considered in equipment utilization, which resulted in the overestimation of equipment utilization. OEE can be considered to combine the operation, maintenance and management of manufacturing equipment and resources (Dal 1999)[21]. OEE can be defined as "A bottom-up approach where an integrated workforce strives to achieve overall equipment effectiveness by eliminating the six big losses" (Nakajima 1988). "Six big losses" are defined as follows: (i) Equipment failure/breakdown losses are categorized as time losses when productivity is reduced, and quantity losses caused by defective products[20].

(ii) Set-up/adjustment time losses result from downtime and defective products that occur when production of one item ends and the equipment is adjusted to meet the requirements of another item.

(iii) Idling and minor stop losses occur when the production is interrupted by a temporary malfunction or when a machine is idling.

(iv) Reduced speed losses refer to the difference between equipment design speed and actual operating speed.

(v) Reduced yield occurs during the early stages of production from machine start up to stabilization.

(vi) Quality defects and rework are losses in quality caused by malfunctioning production equipment.

The first two big losses are known as downtime losses and are used to help calculate a true value for the availability of a machine. The third and fourth big losses are speed losses that determine the performance efficiency of a machine, i.e. the losses which occur as a consequence operating at less than the optimum conditions. The final two losses are considered to be losses due to defects, the larger the number of defects the lower the quality rate of parts within the factory.

Availability Rate (%) = (Operation time / loading time) x 100

Where Operation time = loading time – down time

Performance Rate (%) = (Net operating rate x Operating speed rate) x 100

Where Net operating rate = (Processed Quantity x Actual cycle time) / Operation time Operating speed rate = Ideal cycle time / Actual cycle time

Quality Rate = (Total quantity produced – Quantity scrapped) / (Total quantity produced) x 100

The concept of OEE is becoming increasingly popular and has been widely used as a quantitative tool essential for measurement of productivity[22]. Overall equipment effectiveness (OEE) is used as a key performance indicator for the manufacturing industry in its continuous search for new ways to reduce downtime, costs and waste, to operate more efficiently, and to achieve greater capacity. OEE is a measurement tool to evaluate equipment corrective action methods and ensure permanent productivity improvement. OEE can be used as a 'benchmark' for measuring the initial performance of a manufacturing plant in its entirety. In this manner the initial OEE measure can be compared with future OEE values, thus quantifying the level of improvement made[8]. A practical analysis of operational performance measurement in an automotive industry and the potential benefits of developing OEE as an operational measure have been presented. A new loss classification by Jeong and Phillips (2001)[6] scheme for computing the overall equipment effectiveness is presented for capital intensive industry. Based on the proposed loss classification scheme, a new interpretation of OEE including state analysis, relative loss analysis, lost unit analysis and product unit analysis is attempted. A methodology is presented for constructing a data collection system and developing the total productivity improvement visibility system to implement the proposed OEE and related analyses.

Kwon and Lee (2004) proposed a new methodology to calculate the total saving monetary amount composed of contribution profit and saving costs that are obtained by improving the overall equipment efficiency of processing type equipment[12]. Nachiappan and Anantharaman (2006) presented an approach to measure the overall line effectiveness (OLE) in continuous line-manufacturing system. de Ron and Rooda (2006) revealed that OEE is key performance measure in mass production environments and proposed a performance measure E(Equipment Effectiveness) for standalone equipment, isolated from the environment[23]. Wang (2006) recommended OEE metric as an indicator of the reliability of the production system. A comparison between the expected and current OEE measures provided the much-needed impetus for the manufacturing organizations to improve the maintenance policy and affect continuous improvements in the manufacturing systems. Muchiri and Pintelon (2008) emphasized that the quest for improving productivity in the current global competitive environment has led to the need for rigorously defined performance-measurement systems for manufacturing processes[24]. Overall equipment effectiveness is described as one such performance-measurement tool that measures different types of production losses and indicates areas of process improvement. Anvari et al (2010) proposed a new method, overall equipment effectiveness market-based (OEE-MB) for the precise calculation of equipment effectiveness for full process cycle in order to respond to the steel market. A continuous manufacturing systems used within the steel industry which involve different machines and processes that are arranged in a sequence of operations in order to manufacture the products is considered in the study[3].

Reyes et al (2010) considered overall equipment effectiveness and process capability as well-accepted measures of performance for an industry. The study demonstrated the relationship between OEE and process capability and suggested the existence of a "cut-off point" beyond which improvements in process capability have little impact on OEE[22]. Zammori et al (2011) have proposed the use of OEE as a key performance indicator typically adopted to support Lean Manufacturing and Total Productive Maintenance. Zuashkiani et al (2011) have found that the significant returns on small improvements in OEE justify investment in the management of physical assets, but the wide variation of OEE across firms raises a question regarding the differences persist despite a high return on investments to maximize OEE[6].

Chapter 3

Methodology

To achieve the objectives following methodology has been identified

- Step 1:- Collection of maintenance machines data from the existing maintenance department

- Step 2:-Understand the nature of the maintenance and analysis of the data

- Step 3:-Propose a maintenance model that can increase the availability of the machines, decreases the defects and improves the performance of the machine thus improving OEE

- Step 4:-Implementation of the proposed maintenance model and its analysis

Three important issues i.e. availability, quality and performance concerened with OEE has been discussed in this chapter. A study has been carried out to identify the causes determining availability, quality and performance with existing setup. Methodology to improve OEE has been identified and an effort has been done to improve it.

3.1   Availability

Every industry has a fixed production plan and accordingly the facilities (machines, equipments, assembly line and material supply etc) are developed. However due to unseen reasons all the facilities are not available as per plan for production. This decreases the OEE of the industry. Availability is defined as the ratio of run time to planned production time.

Availability = Run Time / Planned Production Time

Run Time is simply Planned Production Time less Stop Time, where Stop Time is defined as all time where the manufacturing process was intended to be running but was not due to Unplanned Stops (e.g., Breakdowns) or Planned Stops (e.g., Changeovers).

Run Time = Planned Production Time − Stop Time

Unplanned (Breakdown) stop time includes planned (changeover) and interruptions.

It is planned to collect data of availability of the existing facilities at Cosma, Sanand an assembly plant.

3.1.1   Data Collection for Down time

Cosma Sanand plant is an ancilliary unit which prepares subassemblies of the cars and supplies to Ford LTD. All the subassembly lines are planned to produce a subassembly in a prescribed take time (60 Seconds). The focus of the study is on seven assembly lines for BIW part and three assembly lines for (FCM, RTB, LCA) for chasis.

It is necessary to obtain the data and carry out a detailed analysis of the top 5 issues that are being faced at Cosma International. Therefore a thorough data was collected about the downtime on BIW line.

Following is the data obtained from the observation of the BIW lines 1 to 7, the details includes the break down occurrences, its corrective action taken, the amount of time the machine was down. These 7 lines includes only three types of machines which are Robots, Projection Welding machine and one rivet machine. Thus all the points will be surrounding these machines only.

Downtime category is divided into 3 classes A, B, C. The C class includes the downtime from 1 to 10 minutes while the B class included the downtime of 10 to 20 minutes while the A class includes the downtime of 20 to 30 minutes.

3.1.2   Total Downtime in BIW

Downtimes due to breaakdowns observed in all the assembly lines in BIW have been tabulated in Table 3.1. The average monthly breakdown in BIW is found to be 79.60 hrs/month with highest breakdown (21.65 hrs/month) in line 4.

On the basis of the data collected we were able to identify the issues which were responsible for the highest down time and its frequency of the error was also studied. So it was clear that the highest downtime was happening at line no 4 as shown in table 3.1.

Table 3.1: Total downtime of BIW (Monthly)

Sr. No	Line No	Hours
1	Line 1	6.08
2	Line 2	18.25
3	Line 3	7.95
4	Line 4	21.65
5	Line 5	9.37
6	Line 6	6.80
7	Line 7	9.5
	Total	79.60

It has been represented as a piechart in figure 3.1

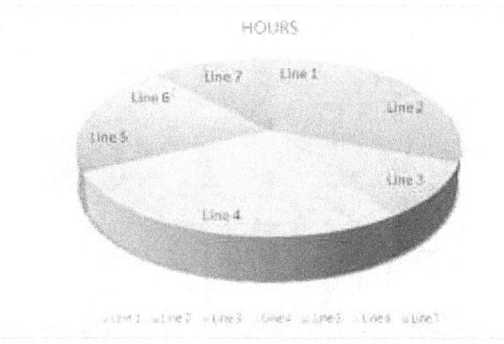

Figure 3.1: Total Downtime BIW in hours (Monthly)

3.1.3 Analysis

During the analysis that had been carried out to know the reason behind sudden breakdowns, it was found that the Preventive maintenance programme was not accurately implemented. The checksheet that were being used were outdated and lacked many key points. So the first step in increasing the availability of the machines included the current checksheet refinement. There are three ways in which the checksheets can be refined.

1. Getting the points from the equipment manuals.

2. Following the Magna Cosma standard.

3. By consulting the experts and selecting the points to be added

Thus we started carrying out the checksheet refinement on 24 different machines as shown in table number 3.2.

Table number 3.2 shows the number of points that have been included based on the three methods on all 24 machines.

The reason behind adding the points is that following these points the preventive maintenance will increase and corrective maintenance will reduce leading to more availability of the machines.

Table 3.2: Checksheet refinement

Sr.no	Name of Equipment	No. of pooints added
1	Mig Welding Robot	12
2	Material handling robot	12
3	Spot Welding Robot	12
4	Stud Welding robot	12
5	Material Handling with Stationary Spot Welding	12
6	Manual Mig Welding Machine	1
7	Projection welding machine	12
8	Nut feeder	12
9	Two way machining centre	23
10	Rivet machine	NA
11	Air hoist and balance	21
12	Diesel generator	23
13	WTP pump	23
14	STP	NA
15	Sectional overhead door	21
16	Dock Lever	24
17	HT Panel	24
18	MLTP	24
19	APFC	7
20	Transformer	17
21	Row power panel	7
22	Mig Welding fixture	NA
23	Spot welding fixure	NA
24	Air Dryer	12

Main issues which were causing the downtime were important to identify, after analyzing the breakdown data of each line whose example is shown in table 3.3 we were able to identify top five issues which are having a major role in the downtime and their frequency is also high.

Table 3.3: Breakdown data

M/C	DT Mins	DT HRS	DT%	Cumm
Robot	150	2.500	41.10	41.10
Sensor	105	1.750	28.77	69.86
Fixture	40	0.667	10.96	80.82
Automation	30	0.500	8.22	89.04
Spot Gun	20	0.333	5.48	94.52
Child part issue	20	0.333	5.48	100.00
Bosch Controller	0	0.000	0.00	100.00
Tip dressing	0	0.000	0.00	100.00
Spatters	0	0.000	0.00	100.00
Spot welding	0	0.000	0.00	100.00
Total	365	6.083	100.00	

The pareto chart for the given table is shown in figure 3.2

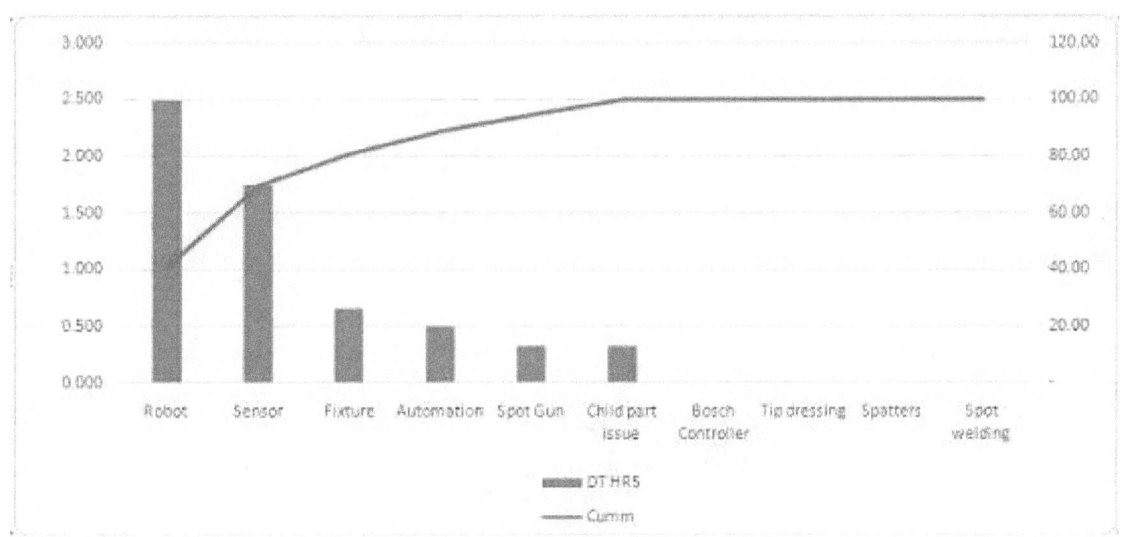

Figure 3.2: Pareto Chart

The major issues are found with the following items.

1. Robot

2. Fixture

3. Sensor

4. Automation (PLC)

5.Childpart

Table 3.4 shows the contribution of each issue in the total downtime

Table 3.4: BIW Top 5 Issues

Issues	Total DT in Min	Percentage	Line 1(Min)	Line 2	Line 3	Line 4	Line 5	Line 6	Line 7
Robot	1417	36	202	120	150	402	201	302	40
Fixture	975	25	150	139	140	200	196	100	50
Sensor	577	14	100	75	50	140	80	82	50
Auto-mation	665	17	95	90	92	120	85	103	80
Child Part	242	6	30	29	25	50	34	32	42

Figure 3.3 shows the pie chart of the given of all the errors in the contribution of the downtime.

From the downtime of the October month, availability of the facilities for all the assembly lines for BIW has been worked out as follows

Availability

= Operating time/Planned production time

=Month October Operating time/ Planned production time

= 720/800

= 90%

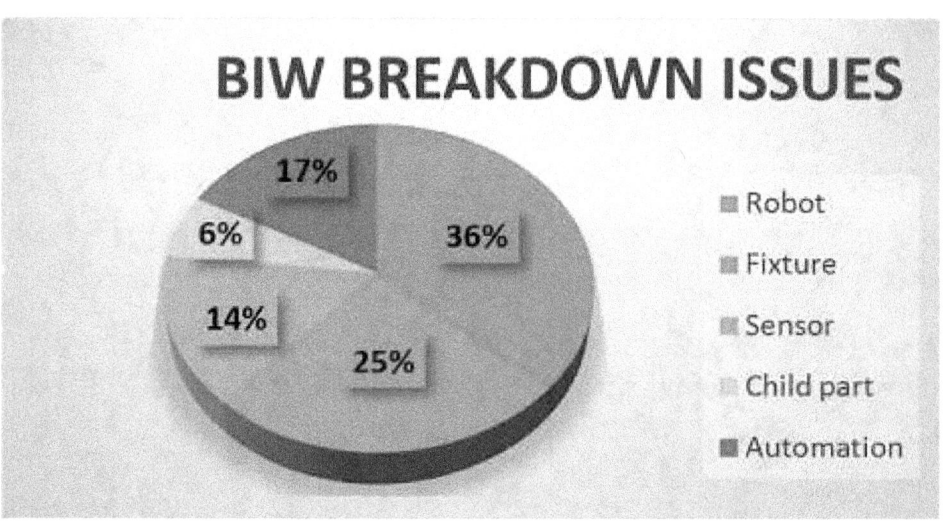

Figure 3.3: Top Five BIW Breakdown Issues

3.1.4 Efforts to improve availability

It has been found that the downtime 80 hours is equivalent to production loss of 4800 assemblies per month and hence loss in business. An attempt has been made to identify the probable causes and has been eliminated for the most influencing issues identified from pareto charts as shown in figure 3.2 discussed in the previous section. It has been explained in the following discussion.

3.1.4.1   Issues with Robot

There were numerous errors which caused robots to stop and hence the cycle.Following errors were identified and measures to eliminate them will be shown.

1. Error 357
2. Tip Dressing
3. Spot miss
4. Force Calibration.

One of the main errors which was displayed in KUKA smart pad was the error 357 which are shown in figure 3.4. These errors indicates the shape variations in the child part which is to be welded. It was observed that the tolerances assigned in the robotic programme were not in correspondence with the parts to be welded. Hence the software was upgraded and the programmed to take the tolerance correponding to part under welding. To remove that, software upgradation was done in which the tolerance limits were given so that the unnecessary stoppages can be avoided.

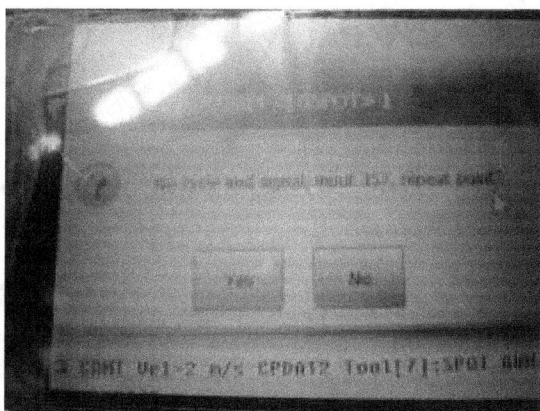

Figure 3.4: Error 357

Another major error was the improper shape of the tip which would stop the robot. Improper shape was found due to improper selection of dressing cutter. The dressing cutter KTW 13 was in use. This was replaced by cutter KTW12 as shown in figure 3.5. The tip shape with cutter KTW12 was tested and no error in robot function was noticed.

Figure 3.5: Tip Dressing Cutter (KTW 12)

"Spot miss" error was also observed which is related to quality. "Spot miss" arises when the robot misses the spot due to technical malfunction of the hardware. To eliminate this, spot counter has been deployed which would compare the number of spots with the given data as shown in figure 3.6.

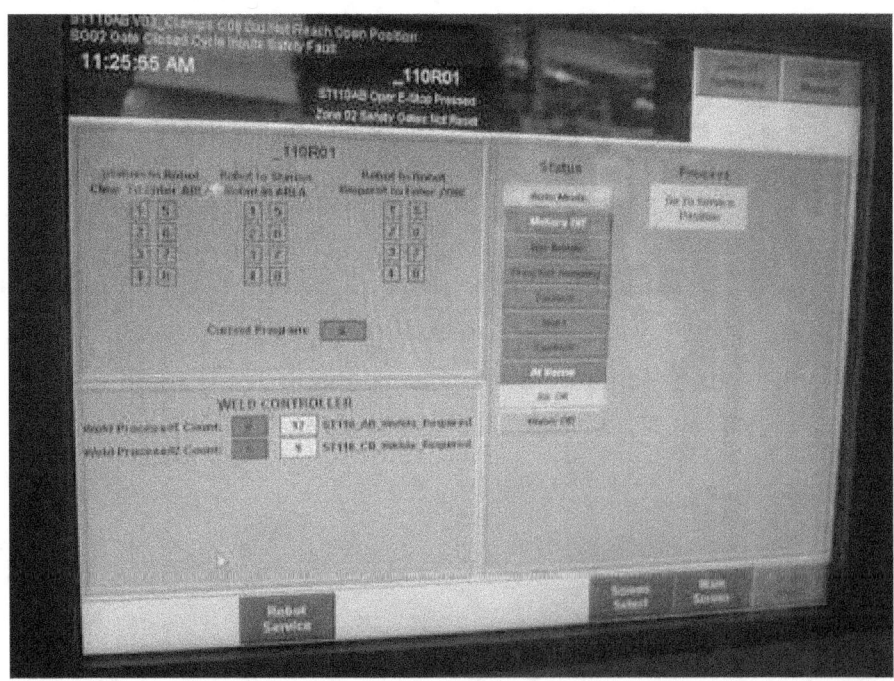

Figure 3.6: Spot Counter

Several times the robot stops due to different amount of force being deployed by the gun than the allowed limit. So force calibration as shown in the figure 3.7 on all the gun was carried out. So malfunctions of the robot can be avoided.

Figure 3.7: Force Gun Calibration

3.1.4.2 Issues with Fixture

Fixture is used to locate the part to be welded precisely and rigidly so that quality mass production can be achieved as shownin figure 3.8. The fixture is facilitated with sensors to check presence of part and position. It has also pneumatic cylinder to hold the part. A welding robot starts spot welding once the "part presence signals" and "hold " signals are received. The sensors generate signals when a part is kept on the fixture. The sensors ensures proper positioning of the parts. Once the part is removed all the signals are degenerated. It had been observed that few signals didnt degenrate even the part had been removed. This is caused due to malfunction of the sensor in the adversed welding atmosphere . Hence even the part is not positioned properly the welding cycle is started as a result of the presence of ghost signal i.e. signal is not degenerated. This leads to erroneous welding assembly and rejection.

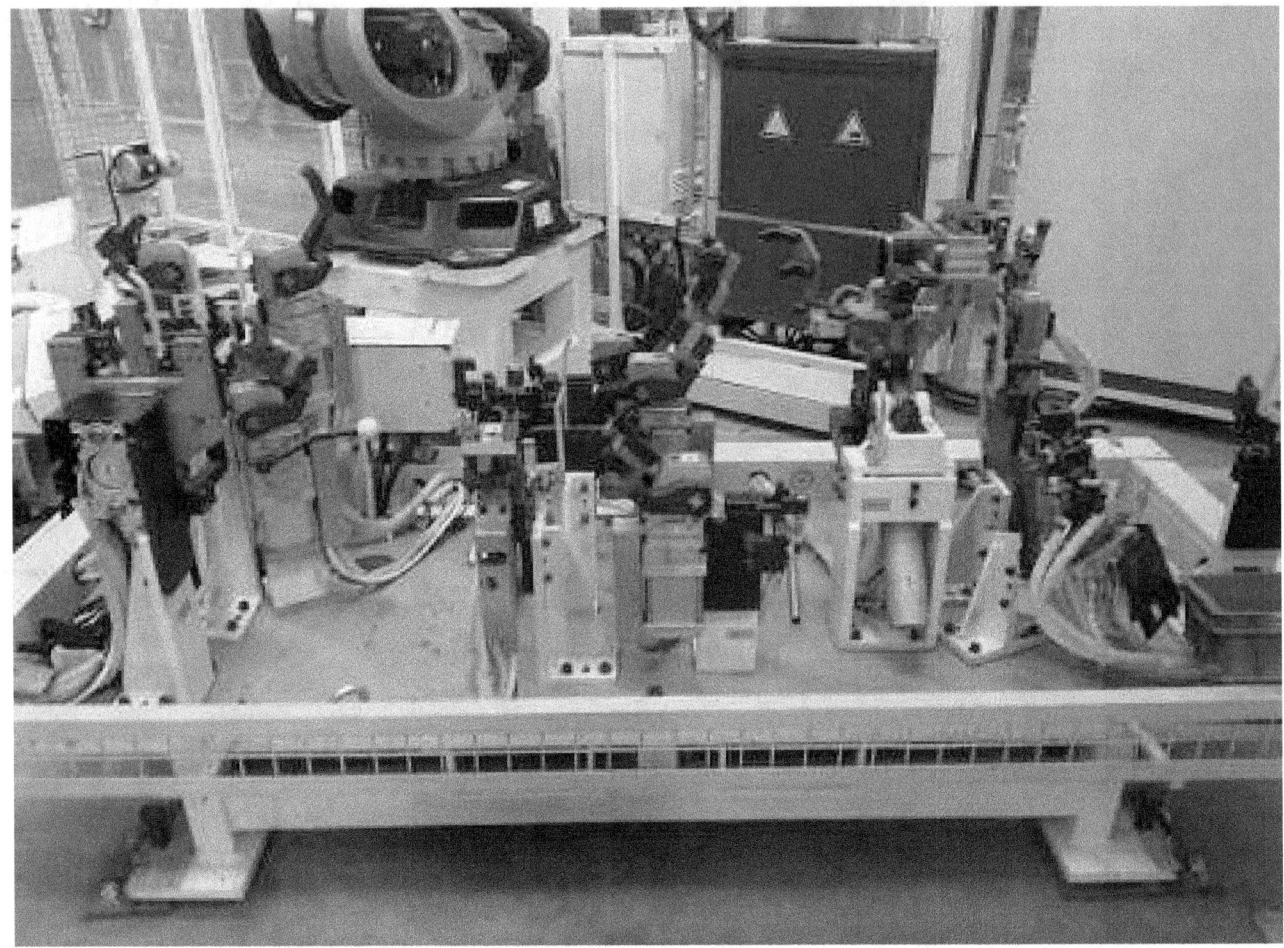

Figure 3.8: Fixture

To solve this issue a "Red Rabbit" poka yoke part has been designed as shown in figure 3.9. This is a dummy part for the part to be welded but with the recess or hole such that the sensors are not covered. When the red rabbit poka yoke part is kept on the fixture no signal should be generated or present. This test ensures all the signals are functionally well. If any signal is detected when "Red rabbit poka yoke" is placed on the fixture, remedial actions are taken by programming & Control team. It is proposed to run "Red rabbit poka yoke " test at the beginning of the shift and every hour so that erroneous welding assembly and rejection can be stopped.

However it needs to be replaced by robust sensors to decrease the downtime resulted from malfunction of sensors.

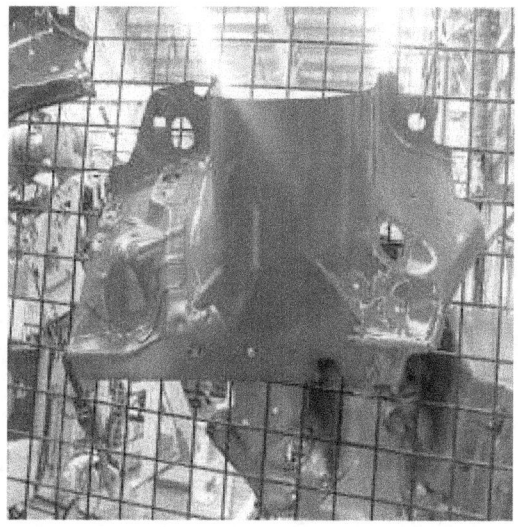

Figure 3.9: Red rabbit poka yoke test

"Poka Yoke" has also been used for full proofing of welding of a nut to sheet metal part fender. This has been termed as part poka yoke as shown in figure 3.10. A fixture has been developed and designed for checking the part geometry as well as the presence of the nut welded in previous operation. A sensor has been deployed in the fixture in the recess corresponding to the nut. When a part with nut welded on it is placed on the fixture, the sensor generates a signal, this ensures no part without nut go for further assembly.

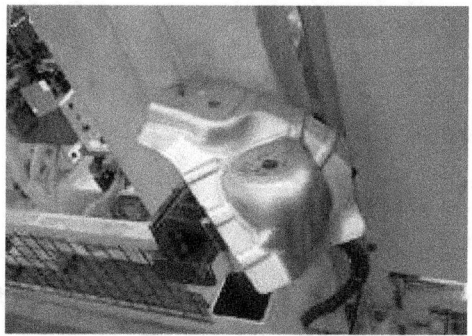

Figure 3.10: Part Poka Yoke

3.1.4.3 Issues with Sensors

Sensors are used extensively on the welding fixture to make full proof the automatic welding process. The welding atmosphere i.e. high temperature and spatter are not conducive for the sensors and frequently causes malfunction. This results in the downtime of the specific machine and station. Effect of spatter on the sensors is shown in figure 3.11(a) which is the present practice .

To eliminate this problems it was analysed if the type and/or location of the sensors can be changed. It has been found that the sensors used to check the clamp(to hold the parts) position can be shifted from fixture to cylinder clamp itself. This removes the sensor from spatter environment. Hence the frequency to change the sensor has dropped down. Morover, the inductive sensors in the spatter environment have been replaced by the reed switch sensors as shown in figure 3.11(b). The reed switch sensors are robust, accurate, long life, reliable and are capable to work in the welding environment. This has led to reduction in the frequency of change of sensors.

It was also analyzed that few inductive sensors in the present practice neither could be shifted to other place nor could be replaced by replaced by reed switch sensors. These sensors are plug and play type. An operator can change the sensor when found malfunctioning. This task has been reassigned to production team (an operator) from the maintenance department. The downtime caused in raising the complaint, waiting for maintenance team can be reduced to much extent. Hence availability of the machine and equipment has improved.

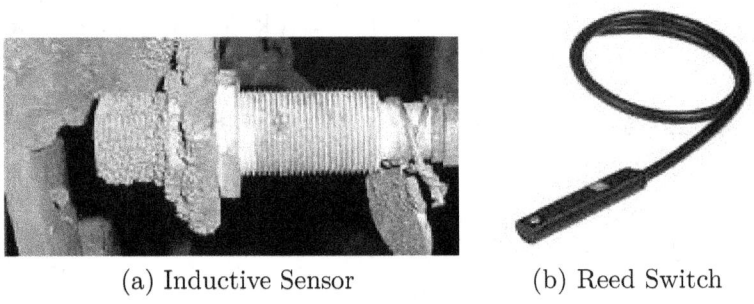

(a) Inductive Sensor   (b) Reed Switch

Figure 3.11: Sensors

3.1.4.4 Miscelleneous issues.

Issues related to retrieval of spares

There are large numbers of machines, equipments and systems which required frequent maintenance and replacement of parts. It is a important role for the preventive maintenance team to raise order, to procure the spares, to store and retrieve as and when need arise.

No systematic approach was followed and as a result a large downtime was observed. Thus it is important that 5S is followed in the stores for the retrieving the spares quickly. Therefore 5S was carried out and the spares were kept in proper order as shown in figure 3.12. A VSRS (Vertical Storage and Retrieval System) has been proposed to handle large number of spares (approximately 500 items). The VSRS is linked with inventory control system. It has been possible to retrieve the required spares on a single entry in the system. This helped to reduce downtime to high extent. The machines/equipment remained down for little time and hence their availability has been increased.

(a) Before   (b) After

Figure 3.12: Storage of materials

Issues related to electrode caps used in projection welding machine

Assemblies have been fabricated using the projection welding machines. The projection weld were found improper and large rejection was beared. After keen observation and analysis it was observed that flatness of electrode cap has great impact on weld quality. Without flatness, electrode cap pressure on the parts to be welded found to be non uniform. This resulted in partial/incomplete projection welds. A nut was pushed in a dry run of projection welding machine with flat and non flat electrode caps. A non flat electrode cap resulted impression at two spots only as shown in figure 3.13(a) whereas the flat electrode produced three impressions as shown in the figure 3.13(b) . This was due to the uniform pressure on all the projections.

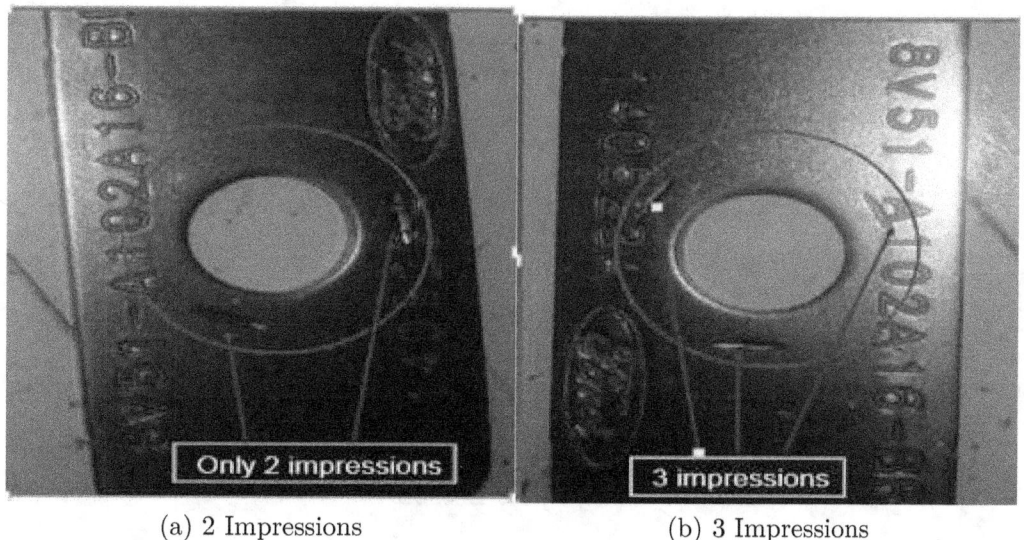

(a) 2 Impressions   (b) 3 Impressions

Figure 3.13: Impressions of the nut

A carbon paper technique has been proposed to check flatness before the projection welding machine started, a white plain paper and a carbon paper is placed under the electrode caps and then a dry run is executed. The impression found on the paper is shown in figure 3.14 (a). With the non flat electrode cap the electrode cap was made flat and a dry run was executed and impression was obtained as shown in figure 3.14 (b). It has been proposed to run this test at every shift of the production. This practice has resulted in almost elimination of the rejections due to improper projection welds

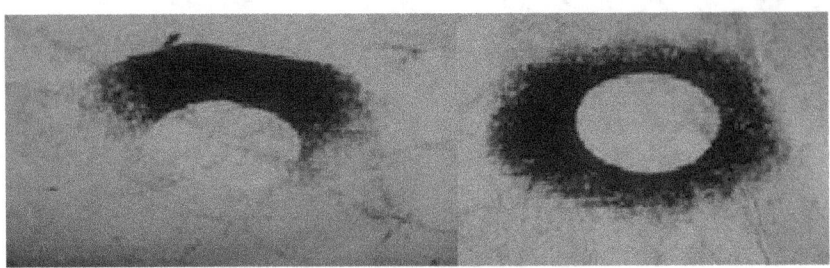

(a) Non flat electrode impression   (b) Flat Electrode Impression

Figure 3.14: Electrode Flatness

Further it was noted that the procedure and the steps involved in using the projection machines was not documented and led to confusion. Thus to solve the problem One Point Lesson (OPL) instruction sheets were created 3.15 which has been made available in 3 languages Hindi, English, Gujarati. The downtime due to improper operation has been reduced as the OPL continously guides the operators.

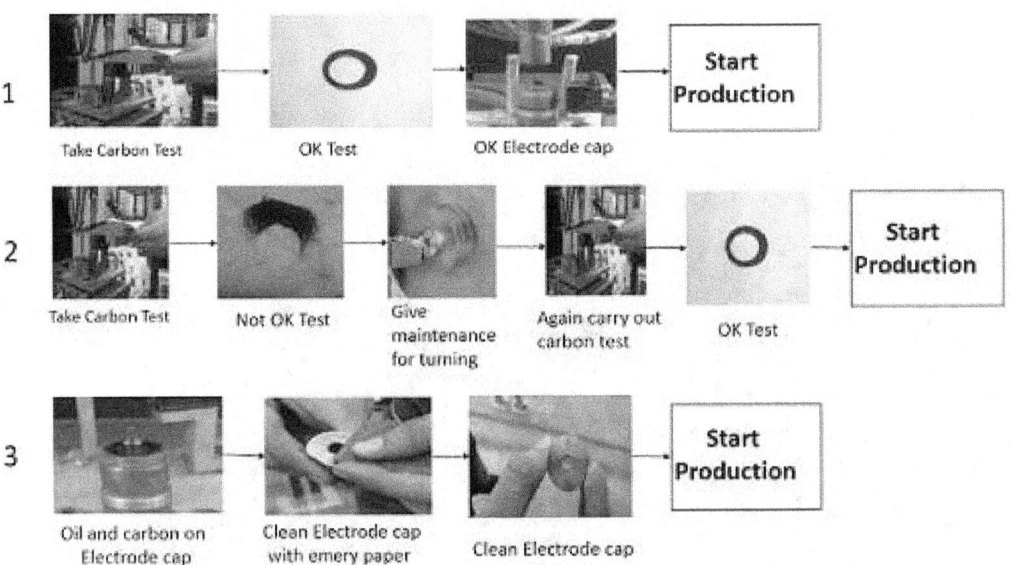

Figure 3.15: One Point Lesson

3.2 Quality

Defects or poor quality of the welded assemblies under the study led to either rework or rejection. It has a great impact on OEE. Poor qualilty means non acceptable appearence and strength of the spot welds. An extensive effort has been made to find nature and occurence of the defects.The defects found in the month of January is found in the table 3.5. The defects observed have been summarised in the table. The possible causes have been also listed in the table after cause and effect analysis.

Table 3.5: Quality Defects

Sr no	Defect	No of occurences	% Occurences	Causes
1	Cracked and ruptured weld	13	0.22	Poor tip condition, Sharp edge on tip face, Hold time too long, Weld force too high, Poor setup of tooling
2	Pitting	20	0.33	Poor tip condition, Squeeze time too short, Dirty and scaly material, Weld force too high, Poor tooling set up
3	Burn holes	22	0.37	Weld current too high, Weld time too long, Poor tip or strip condition, Foreign material jammed into the gap between the layers.
4	Excessive Indentation	12	0.2	Poor tip condition, Weld time too long, Weld force too high, Poor part fit up, Weld current too high

	Skidding			Poor tip condition,Tips misalignment, Tips at angle to the metal Guns are loose Excessive tip
5		17	0.28	force
	Surface Expulsion			Squeeze time too short, Weld force too low, Tips face too small, Tips misalignment, Weld current/time
6		15	0.25	too high
	Interface Expulsion			Poor Tip Condition, Dirty material, Weld force too low, Squeeze time too short, Weld
7		10	0.2	current too high
	No Weld			Poor tip condition,Weld time too, short Weld force too high Weld current too low Poor electrical
8		0	0	connection
	Brassing			Poor tip dressing, Weld force too low, Weld current too high, Weld time too long, Insufficient
9		12	0.2	Cooling

3.2.1 Analysis

The causes for the defects were analysed and the process parameters like weld current, gun force, hold time, squeeze time were set. All other causes were also addressed. The number of defects were decreased but could not be eliminated completely. It was observed that the number of defects increased as the number of spots increased. Hence experiments were carried out to find tip dressing frequency.

3.2.1.1 Tip Change

Tip change is a process in which the tip is changed after several number of spots due to the carbon impurities dust and partial melting the tip gets deformed and partially damaged is needed to be changed so that proper welding is carried out with proper spot nugget diameter.As shown in the 3.16 figure the tip changing procedure is shown.

It is imperative that the proper tip changing cycles is decided so that the spot quality can be improved.

 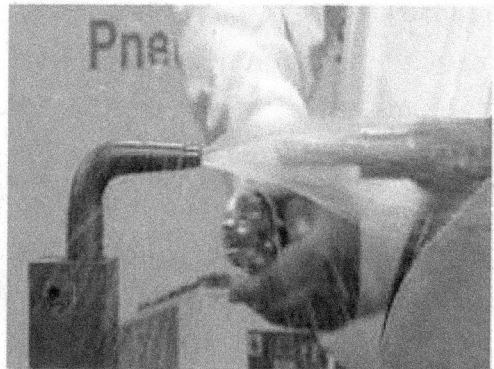

Figure 3.16: Tip change

3.2.1.2 Tip Dressing

Tip dressing is a process in which the robot goes to the tip dresser where the tip dresser dresses the tip i.e it sharpens the tip like a sharpener thus removing the carbon and other impurities. Therefore the same tip can be used to do the spot welding just by keeping the nugget diameter in the range and thus it can be used several times before tip change.The difference can be seen in the tips as shown in the figure 3.16 where (a) shows the tip before getting dressed and (b) shows the tip after getting dressed.

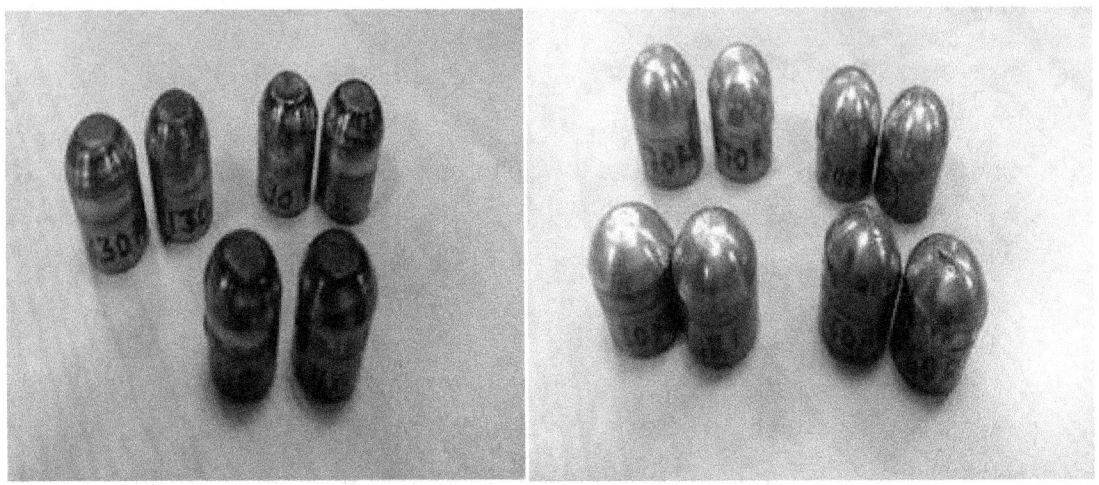

(a) Before Tip Dressing   (b) After Tip Dressing

Figure 3.17: Tip Dressing

3.2.1.3 Experiment to find tip dressing and tip change frequency.

To find the frequency of tip dressing and tip change spots were made on the sheet and the nugget diameter was mesured after every spot weld. The results are shown in figure 3.18 . It can be seen that as the number of spots increases the nugget diameter also increases.

The acceptable nugget diameter is (7 ± 0.5mm). It has been observed that after 150 spots, the nugget diameter is not acceptable. Hence tip dressing is recommended. The experiments were continued after redressing of the tip. It was observed that after redressing the tip can produce 150 acceptable spots i.e. nugget diameter is with in permissible values. However after 2 redressing i.e. total 450 spots the size of the tip didnt calibrated the robot positioning during the mastering process.ie. Referencing. Hence it was concluded that the tip should be changed or replaced after two redressing or 450 number of spots.

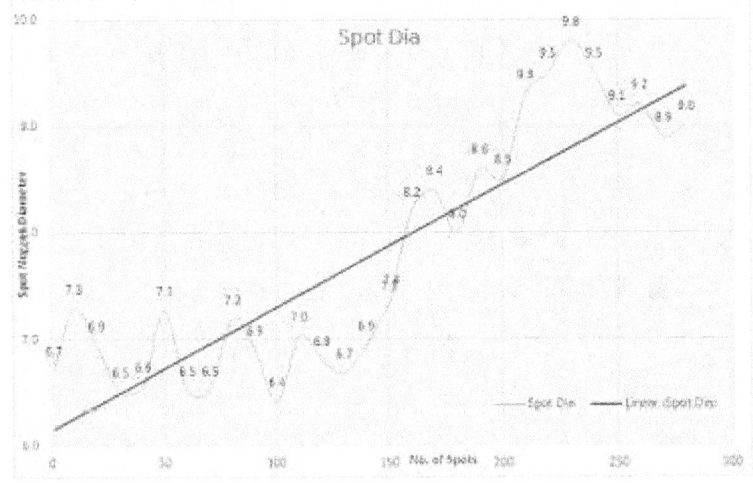

Figure 3.18: Nugget diameter vs Spot diameter

3.2.1.4 Spot Counter

To calculate these spots and keep its track, Spot Counter a programme counting the number of spots was deployed on all stations and a acknowledge button was added in HMI as shown in figure 3.19.

In the spot counter programme the spots being taken are compared with the actual number of spots that are fed into the programme. If the spots are not equal to the predefined number of spots than the line gets stopped and the part is restricted from going ahead. In the figure 3.19 the screen of HMI is shown in which the spot counter programme is shown.

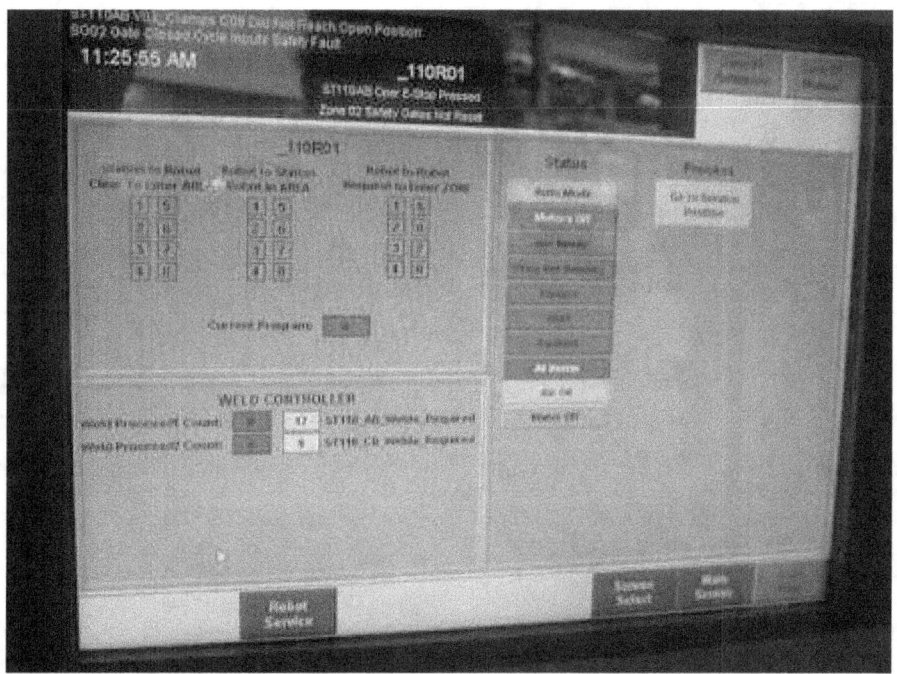

Figure 3.19: Spot Counter

Thus these were the various methods and concepts that were used to reduce the defects in the parts which inturn can increase the overall equipment effectiveness.

3.3 Performance

Performance takes into account anything that causes the manufacturing process to run at less than the maximum possible speed when it is running (including both Slow Cycles and Small Stops).

It is calculated as:

Performance = (Total count / Run time) / Ideal run rate

3.3.1 Performance in the month of February

Performance of the machine is one of the most important factor to be considered as the performance is the factor where there lies a lot of scope of improvement. The main percentage can be highly affected by improving this area. Thus we calculated the JPH (Jobs per hour) of the month January as shown in the table 3.6.

Table 3.6: JPH in month of February

Sr no	AREA	JPH
1	Front rail Line 3	52
2	A pillar outer	52
3	Front rail Line 2	51
4	Rear rail RH line	50
5	Rear rail LH line	43

After studying different lines and stations we shortlisted top five stations having the lowest JPH and we set the target to get its JPH higher.Thus to increase the performance of the machine various new methods and techniques needed to be devised. KAIZEN being one of them. As shown in the table 3.6 the JPH of the month of February is shown which are quite less due to which there is a considerable decrease in the performance percentage and subsequent OEE percentage.

3.3.2 KAIZEN

Following are the different KAIZEN activities that were being used in order to increase the JPH and its description is shown below.

1. Spot Sequence alteration

2. Path optimization

3. Spot Shifting

4. Logic Modification

5. Tip Dresser relocation

3.3.2.1 Spot Sequence Alteration: -

In this process the spot sequence is changed so that the required number of spots can be made in the least possible time thus increasing the JPH.

In the figure 3.20 it is shown the two sequnces of the spot welding one being the previous sequence and one the new sequence.

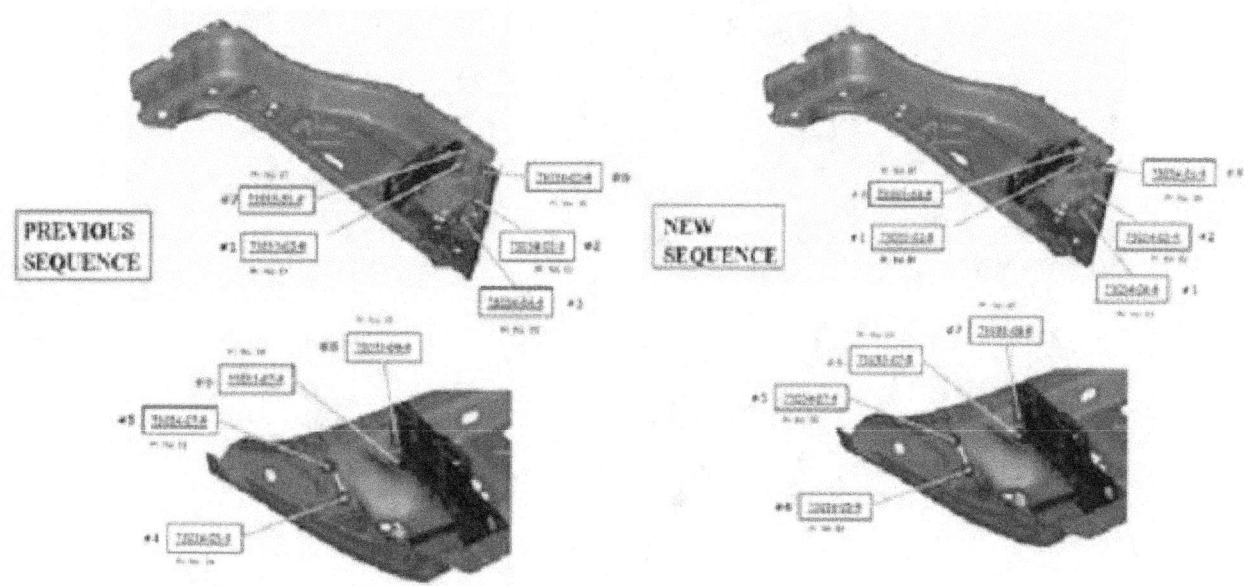

Figure 3.20: Previouse and new spot sequences

3.3.2.2 Path Optimization:

It is a process in which the path of the robot travelling is optimized in other words the travelling path of the robot is so selected that it travels the maximum spot distance in minimum time.

3.3.2.3 Spot shifting

Spot shifting is a process in which the spot is so shifted that it does not affect the strength of the assembly and at the same time removes the unnecessary spot from the assembly giving it a reducing cycle time by 3.5 seconds.

3.3.2.4 Logic Modification:-

In the case of logic modification the plc programmers modifies the program of the controller in such a way that the useless commands are dumped and only useful commands gets executed thus resulting in the reducing cycle time by 4 seconds.

3.3.2.5 Tip dresser relocation:

In the case of the relocation of the tip dresser what happens is that the location of the tip dresser is so located that the robot travelling path is shot when it goes for tip dressing thus reducing the take time by 1.5 seconds as shown in figure 3.21.

Thus due to all this kaizen activities the result is that it that there is an increase in the JPH which leads to overall increase in the percentage of the performance.

Figure 3.21: Tip dresser relocation

Thus these were the various methods and concepts that were used to increase the performance of the machine which inturn can increase the overall equipment effectiveness.

Chapter 4

Results and Discussions

After deploying all the concepts, methods and strategies we were able to get the following results.

4.1 Availability

Different concepts and techniques were approached and employed to enhance the Corrective maintenance and Preventive Maintenance in the plant and the main objective to reduce the corrective maintenance and increase the preventive maintenance is still being done by employing different techniques and concepts as discussed in previous chapters. Secondly the main task of generating the preventive maintenance points as per scheduled time was developed and implemented.

After all these activities we were able to get the following results as shown in table 4.1

Here the downtime hours of the october month is shown in comparison with the down time hours of November after deploying all the techniques.

Table 4.1: Comparison of Downtime Hours

Month	OCT	Month	NOV
Line No	HRS	Line No	HRS
Line 1	6.08	Line 1	12.53
Line 2	18.25	Line 2	11.13
Line 3	7.95	Line 3	4.68
Line 4	21.65	Line 4	9.00
Line 5	9.37	Line 5	9.72
Line 6	6.80	Line 6	6.27
Line 7	9.50	Line 7	7.27
Total	79.60	Total	60.60

As shown in table 4.1 the statistics of the month October is shown in comparison with the month of November. Thus employing these techniques, concepts and methods maintenance team was able to reduce the downtime of the 7 BIW lines from 80 hours to 60 hours that is reduction of 25 % in the break down time which saves around **20** production hours. Thus we were able to increase preventive maintenance in such a way that we reduced breakdown maintenance by **25%**.

OEE Calculation (Availability) Availability = Operating time/Planned production time

Month October Operating time/ Planned production time = 720/800= **90%**

Month November Operating time/ Planned production time = 740/800= **92.5%**

4.2   Quality

After determining the proper tip change and tip dress sequences they were deployed and its result were seen as shown in table 4.2.

Table 4.2: Comparison of monthly defects

(a) February

Month	Feb
M/C	No. of occurrences
Burn holes	2
Pitting	2
Skidding	1
Surface Expulsion	1
Cracked and ruptured Weld	2
Excessive Indentation	2
Brassing	1
Interface Expulsion	Total 13

(b) January

Month	Jan
M/C	No. of occurrences
Burn holes	22
Pitting	20
Skidding	17
Surface Expulsion	15
Cracked and ruptured Weld	13
Excessive Indentation	12
Brassing	12
Interface Expulsion	Total 121

Quality

= Good Count / Total Count

34

Month January

(6000-121)/6000

= 0.97*100

= **97%**

MonthFebruary

(6600-13)/6600

= 0.99*100

= **99%**

4.3 Performance

Different kind of KAIZEN activities were being followed which resulted in the following results as shown in Table 4.3.

Table 4.3: KAIZEN activities

KAIZEN				
Sr no	AREA	JPH Before Kaizen	JPH After Kaizen	Kaizen Activities
1	Front rail	52	55	Spot Sequence altered
2	A pillar outer	52	55	Path optimization, Spot shifting, Logic modification, Relocating tip dresser
3	Front rail	51	54	Path optimization, Spot shifting, Logic modification, Relocating tip dresser
4	Rear rail RH line	50	54	5 Rear rail LH line 43 46 Spot Sequence altered

Month February Performance

= (Total count / Run time) / Ideal run rate

= (370*20)/ (20*8*60)/1

=**77 %**

Month March Performance

$= \text{(Total count / Run time) / Ideal run rate}$

$= (386*20)/ (20*8*60)/1$

$= \mathbf{80\%}$

Thus these were the results of all the three factors of OEE at different times taken during the project duration.

4.4 Results

Now the main focus is to look at the all the three factors at the same time i.e. month, so that the overall equipment effectiveness can be obtained in a given month.

Thus OEE was calculated for the month of October 2015 to April 2016 as shown in the below table 4.4

Table 4.4: Monthly OEE

	OCT	NOV	DEC	JAN	FEB	MARCH	APRIL
Availability	90	92.5	92	92.5	93	93	93
Quality	95	96	97	97	99	99	99
Performance	65	68	75	76	77	80	80
OEE	**55%**	**60%**	**67%**	**67%**	**70%**	**73%**	**73%**

The total improvement of OEE from the month when TPM practises were being deployed (October) to the final month when all the TPM practises were implemented is shown in the figure 4.1.Thus showing OEE before and after implementation of TPM.

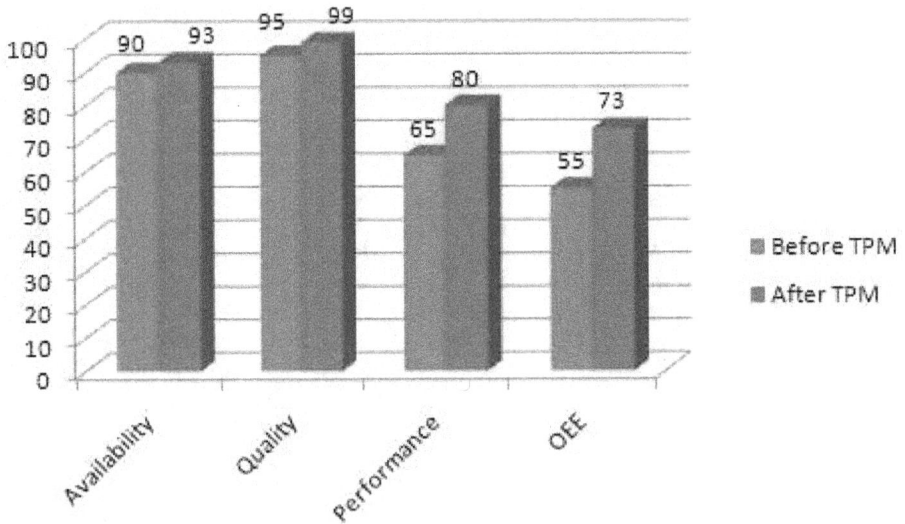

Figure 4.1: TPM Comparison

Chapter 5

Conclusion and Future Scope

5.1   Conclusion

Following conclusion is derived from implementation of TPM in an automotive company:

1. Success of TPM depends on various pillars like 5-S, Jishu Hozen, Planned Maintenance, Quality maintenance, Kaizen, Office TPM and Safety, Health & Environment.

2. Overall Equipment Effectiveness has improved from **55% to 73%** indicating the improvement in availability from **90 to 93**, quality from **95 to 99** and performance from **65 to 80**.

3. A great scope of improvement in the OEE percentage can be seen in the performance factor, increasing that can get the company at par with world class OEE percentage.

4. The key factors for this implementation are workers involvement and top management support.

5. Still world class TPM implementation is possible with continual support at all the levels along with the supply of necessary resources.

5.2   Future Scope

- Future research may be done to explore the dynamics of translating equipment effectiveness or loss of effectiveness in terms of cost.

- Various different technologies and tools can be used to enhance the OEE process like

1. Computerized Maintenance Management System (CMMS)

2. Manufacturing Execution System (MES)

3. Statistical Process Contro (SPC)

4. Fault Detection and Classification (FDC)

References

1. Mike Bourne*. Researching performance measurement system implementation: the dynamics of success and failure. *Production Planning & Control*, 16(2):101–113, 2005.

2. Erik Adolfsson and Dahlström Tuvstarr. Efficiency in corrective maintenance-a case study at skf gothenburg. 2011.

3. Rachna Shah and Peter T Ward. Lean manufacturing: context, practice bundles, and performance. *Journal of operations management*, 21(2):129–149, 2003.

4. Hans-Dieter Zollondz. *Lexikon Qualitätsmanagement: Handbuch des Modernen Managements auf der Basis des Qualitätsmanagements–Edition Versicherungsmanagement*. Walter de Gruyter GmbH & Co KG, 2000.

5. Hongye Wang. *A Unified Methodology of Maintenance Management for Repairable Systems Based on Optimal Stopping Theory*. PhD thesis, Southern University, 2008.

6. Laura Swanson. An empirical study of the relationship between production technology and maintenance management. *International Journal of Production Economics*, 53(2):191–207, 1997.

7. Inderpreet P Singh Ahuja and Jaimal Singh Khamba. Total productive maintenance: literature review and directions. *International Journal of Quality & Reliability Management*, 25(7):709–756, 2008.

8. K Arunraj and M Maran. A review of tangible benefits of tpm implementation. *International Journal of Applied Science and Engineering Research*, 3(1):171–176, 2014.

9. Adnan Hj Bakri, Abdul Rahman Abdul Rahim, Noordin Mohd Yusof, and Ramli Ahmad. Boosting lean production via tpm. *Procedia-Social and Behavioral Sciences*, 65:485–491, 2012.

10. Abhijeet K Digalwar and Padma V Nayagam. Implementation of total productive maintenance in manufacturing industries: A literature-based metadata analysis. *IUP Journal of Operations Management*, 13(1):39, 2014.

11. Andrew Ginder, Alan Robinson, and Charles J Robinson. *Implementing TPM: The North American Experience*. CRC Press, 1995.

12. Fatih Hayat. The effects of the welding current on heat input, nugget geometry, and the mechanical and fractural properties of resistance spot welding on mg/al dissimilar materials. *Materials & Design*, 32(4):2476–2484, 2011.

13. Abhishek Jain, Rajbir Bhatti, Harwinder Singh Deep, and SK Sharma. Implementation of tpm for enhancing oee of small scale industry. *International Journal of IT, Engineering and Applied SciencesResearch*, 1, 2012.

14. Ki-Young Jeong and Don T Phillips. Operational efficiency and effectiveness measurement. *International Journal of Operations & Production Management*, 21(11): 1404–1416, 2001.

15. Nagaraj H Kamath and Lewlyn LR Rodrigues. A pilot study for total production management in printing industry. *Indian Journal of Applied Research*, 4(12):476–479, 2014.

16. Ravishankar V Korgal and Anil S Badiger. Application of tpm in engineering education: Literature overview.

17. Fang Lee Cooke. Implementing tpm in plant maintenance: some organisational barriers. *International Journal of Quality & Reliability Management*, 17(9):1003–1016, 2000.

18. Ohwoon Kwon and Hongchul Lee. Calculation methodology for contributive managerial effect by oee as a result of tpm activities. *Journal of quality in Maintenance Engineering*, 10(4):263–272, 2004.

19. Fakhraddin Maroofi. Total productive maintenance for modeling the enablers in the performing of ism access. *International Research Journal of Applied and Basic Sciences*, 6(8):1161–1174, 2013.

20. Kathleen E McKone, Roger G Schroeder, and Kristy O Cua. Total productive maintenance: a contextual view. *Journal of operations management*, 17(2):123–144, 1999.

21. CA Voss. Operations management–from taylor to toyota–and beyond? *British Journal of Management*, 6(s1):S17–S29, 1995.

22. Kanwarpreet Singh. Manufacturing performance enhancement through total quality management and total productive maintenance paradigms. 2015.

23. Aditya Parida and Uday Kumar. Maintenance performance measurement (mpm): issues and challenges. *Journal of Quality in Maintenance Engineering*, 12(3):239–251, 2006.

24. Yash Parikh and Pranav Mahamuni. Total productive maintenance: Need & framework. 2015.

www.ingramcontent.com/pod-product-compliance
Lightning Source LLC
Chambersburg PA
CBHW052042280526
45791CB00010B/3046